GRANT WEST:
LEARNING THROUGH MUSIC

TRISTAN HITCHENS-BROOKINS

Text Copyright © 2025 Planting People Growing Justice Press
Illustrations copyright © 2025 Planting People Growing Justice Press

Cover Artwork and Illustrations by Whimsical Designs by CJ
Design by Reyhana Ismail

All rights reserved.

No part of this book may be reproduced in any manner without express written consent of the publisher, except in the case of brief excerpts in critical reviews and articles.

All inquiries or sales request should be addressed to:

Planting People Growing Justice Press
P.O. Box 131894
Saint Paul, MN 55113
www.ppgjli.org

Printed and bound in the United States of America
First Edition
LCCN: 2024951706
1-9781959223696/9798896050025-04/15/2025

DEDICATION
To Mimi, thank you for everything you've done.

TABLE OF CONTENTS

Introduction
The Star Emerges 5

Chapter 1:
The Sound of Inspiration 7

Chapter 2:
St. Paul's Man of Action 13

Chapter 3:
Dreams Coming to Reality 18

Chapter 4:
The Legacy of a Local Legend 23

Ways to Make a Difference 26

About the Author 28

Glossary 29

Source Notes, Books, Websites 30

Words in **bold** are in the glossary.

THE STAR EMERGES

Grant had always loved music. Ever since he was little, Grant would sit at the piano. With his fingers dancing across the keys, he created melodies that made everyone around him smile. By the time he turned 18, Grant was ready to share his music with the world. So, when he was invited to play at a big music show at Garveya's, the most popular music store in town, he was thrilled.

With a deep breath, Grant began to play. First, he played old, classic tunes that echoed through the store. The crowd leaned in because they were excited by the familiar songs. "Play more, Grant!" they cheered, clapping their hands in excitement. Their energy fueled Grant's confidence. He smiled and began playing lively, new songs he knew by heart. The music flowed effortlessly, and for the first time, Grant felt like a true musician. It was a day he would never forget.

Grant grew up to be a music teacher and a community leader. He helped many children discover joy in learning music.

CHAPTER 1:
THE SOUND OF INSPIRATION

On July 14, 1946, Thomas Arthur and Corine Virginia West welcomed Grant into the world. Grant is the eldest of three children. He had two younger brothers named Barry and Tom. His family lived in a small town in Wyoming called Cheyenne. There were not many Black people there. He liked to play with his friends, and they created toy cars out of wood and nails.

Grant discovered a love for music at an early age. At only 8 years old, Grant began playing the piano and entertaining guests at his grandma's soul food restaurant and cafe, "The Black and Tan." His grandmother, Vera Stella, saw Grant's talent and creativity. She helped him gain the confidence to play in front of crowds and try new music.

Grant enjoyed playing music with his family. His parents possessed a natural musical talent, which they taught to their children. His mother had a beautiful singing voice. She told Grant to play the piano every day. She often reminded him: "Practice makes perfect." His father was known for skillfully playing the trumpet. He helped Grant learn to love music.

Grant and Barry aspired to be the best musicians in the world. They often competed with one another. They also taught Tom how to play instruments.

Grant's parents taught his family to work hard and overcome challenges. Grant's father worked as a laborer in construction and sanitation engineering. His mother worked as a **stenographer** for the Warren Air Force Base. Grant saw how hard they worked every day. This taught him to work hard too.

From a young age, Grant learned that his father's family had been enslaved by the Cherokee tribe. After the Civil War was over and slavery was legally abolished, his ancestors fled their homes due to the violence of the Ku Klux Klan. They migrated north and settled in the Midwest. Grant learned that Black people faced injustices for centuries. They had to work harder than others to do well.

COMMUNITY HISTORIAN

Arturo Alfonso Schomburg was a Puerto Rican man of African and German descent. He researched and published the accomplishments of Afro-Latinos and African Americans across the globe. His work led to the archive of history and information about people of African descent called the Schomburg Center for Research in Black Culture.

This made Grant respect Black people for their determination and dedication.

Grant's school did not teach him about the accomplishments of Black people, but his family's story made him eager to learn more. He spent time in the library reading about Black history and culture. When Grant grew up, he wanted to help make things fair for everyone. He worked to make Black communities stronger by protecting their rights and creating access to opportunities. His family history planted a seed in him that would later grow into working to fight racial injustice.

Grant's music teacher, Ms. Daisy Bates, moved his heart and made him the musician he is today. She taught him to play the piano and showed him that he had a special gift to share with the world. She even noticed Grant could do something special. He could hear any musical sound and play it on the piano by ear. This is a rare gift called **perfect pitch.** Perfect pitch is like having special ears that can tell just by listening what note a piano or any instrument is playing.

Ms. Bates thought Grant could be a great musician one day. She told him to keep practicing. She believed he could do more than just what he learned in school.

This made Grant feel good about himself and built his confidence. He started to believe in his skills and develop them. Grant liked music so much that he decided he wanted to be a music teacher when he grew up. He wanted to inspire students to grow through music.

FACT:

There were five tribes of Native Americans who owned slaves in the nineteenth century: the Choctaws, Chickasaws, Creeks, Seminoles, and the Cherokee. The Cherokee owned more slaves than the others and often used the Africans as a bridge to connect to white society.

CHAPTER 2:
ST. PAUL'S MAN OF ACTION

In 1966, Grant left Wyoming and moved to Saint Paul, Minnesota. Grant felt amazed by the number of Black people in one place. But that was not all he felt. He saw that their community was in dire need of help. Many families struggled to meet their basic needs, some could not afford proper housing, and others needed better education in school. Grant remembered what his parents had taught him about the importance of service. He decided to take action.

Grant got a job at the St. Paul Urban League, where he helped Black families find **affordable** homes. He also taught music to Black children in churches to improve their education. This was a way to connect the community to arts and culture. While doing this work, Grant performed with a legendary pop and jazz singer named Sammy Davis Jr.

During this time, Grant learned that the government was not treating Black people fairly, especially in housing and schools. Grant saw that some places would not let Black families rent or buy homes. Some areas were **segregated** and would not allow Black people to live there. This taught him that advocating for fairness and justice is very difficult. It would require hard work, dedication, and perseverance. Grant's journey to become a musician trained him well for this task. To become a musician good enough to perform with an incredible singer like Sammy, Grant focused on his music every day. He applied that level of discipline to his work serving Black families and became a leader in the Black community of St. Paul.

Grant saw that many Black children did not have access to music education. Again, he decided to take action. He started providing music lessons to

FACT:

The Urban League Twin Cities served the African American community in Minnesota since before 1928. The goal was to provide racial justice to African American communities in the Twin Cities. Today the organization continues to work so African descendants in Minnesota can have their basic needs like food and shelter met.

TRAILBLAZING ENTERTAINER

Sammy Davis Jr. was a talented musician and actor. As a Black man, he faced many challenges because of his race. He worked hard and became one of the most famous musicians ever. He also helped tear down barriers faced by other Black entertainers.

children in St. Paul. He showed children how to play different instruments, but he really loved teaching them to play the piano. Grant taught many styles of music like jazz, classical, and pop music.

Grant had a special way of teaching that inspired his students to do their best and taught them to love creating music. He knew that kids learn in different ways. Some people learn by listening. Some learn by watching. He asked the children what songs they liked. Then, he played those songs and taught the children how to play them too. This helped his students understand how to create, not just memorize music.

FACT: DIVERSITY IN LEARNING STYLES

Human beings learn in different ways. Generally, people are one of four types of learners: visual, auditory, reading or writing, and kinesthetic. Visual learners prefer their eyes, auditory learners listen with their ears, readers or writers learn best by reading or writing, and kinesthetic learners learn by moving their bodies.

CHAPTER 3:
DREAMS COMING TO REALITY

In 1987, Grant met another talented music teacher, Carl Walker. They both taught music lessons in Saint Paul to local Black children. Grant and Carl dreamed of starting a school. They knew that together they could reach more students and have a greater impact. They felt inspired by the African proverb: "If you want to go fast, go alone. If you want to go far, go together."

In 1988, Grant and Carl opened a music school, Walker West Music Academy. They wanted to teach their community about music history and culture. Their school helped the community connect to the arts through music. Children from across the state wanted to learn at Walker West. Grant's dream had come true because he was providing music education to many students.

Grant trained his students to become **leaders**. He wanted to help them grow as people, so he used music as a tool to teach important life skills.

He taught students key skills like **critical thinking** and problem solving. Grant wanted all the students at Walker West to love learning music and become people who could help others.

Grant also thought it was important for his students to know how sounds and rhythm work together to create music. He used this experience to teach teamwork. He not only taught them to read music or play instruments, but he also taught them to respect music as an art. Art is a tool for self-expression and cultural appreciation. The students used art to create music and celebrate music from around the world.

FACT:

Walker West Music Academy is a non-profit community school that teaches music of all styles, including classical, jazz, and other improvisational music lessons to the youth and adults in the Twin Cities. It is also the first and oldest music education institution in the United States founded by Black people.

Grant believed teaching his students to respect music was the best way to help them learn. He knew it would make them excited about music and eager to explore new ideas and concepts.

Grant faced some big problems when he started Walker West. He wanted to teach music to kids, but he also had to run the school as a **business**. There was not enough space for all the students to learn. Some families did not have enough money to pay for music lessons. The academy needed a permanent home and money to cover lessons.

Grant and Carl searched for a new place for the school and found a closed-down barbeque restaurant on Selby Avenue. It was the only available location they could afford. They bought it but could not pay anyone to clean the building. Grant and Carl cleaned the whole building by themselves. They loved teaching their students and helping their community so much that they cleaned every drop of grease out of the carpets.

Grant wanted to help everyone learn music. He made agreements with the parents. If they could not pay, they could help in other ways. When Grant needed help turning the restaurant into a school, he made a deal with a worker. They decided that in exchange for his help, Grant would teach his daughter enough lessons to perform at Carnegie Hall.

Grant tried to teach his students a lot of music in a short time. He wanted every kid to learn as much as they could. That way, all the kids could learn about music, even if they could not pay for lessons over a long period of time.

CHAPTER 4:
THE LEGACY OF A LOCAL LEGEND

Throughout his life, Grant served his community. He used music as a tool to make St. Paul, the Black community, and the world a better place. He lived as a teacher, leader, husband, father, brother, and community advocate. His work influenced music culture in St. Paul, leading his students down a path of success.

Walker West students are all over the world. Many live as famous musicians. Some students played on national stages like the White House. Some current students even played in international **venues**, while others are political leaders, lawyers, engineers, and doctors. Grant's life significantly improved the lives of thousands of people and every single person he ever met.

Grant is committed to helping every student grow through music. He envisions a world where

students imagine, create, and build a better future. He also wants everyone to enjoy music. It does not matter who they are. Music helped Grant grow up and be a great leader and effective changemaker in his community. He believes everyone should get to play music to experience the same opportunity. Each person should learn how amazing music can be.

Music can uplift a person and a community. Music can inspire change and action in a person's life. Most importantly, music can bring people together, and Grant believes that unity is important. Unity allows communities to stay strong, respect one another, and create a healthy, positive culture. Grant worked to create that kind of culture in St. Paul, and he succeeded.

"Music is a paradigm we use at Walker West Music Academy for teaching success. Everyone wants to be successful. When a student is inspired, you can't keep them from learning."

WAYS TO MAKE A DIFFERENCE

- **Don't be afraid to try something new.** Grant West made a difference because he wasn't afraid to do things he had never done before.

- **Look for ways to share kindness and teach others something you've learned.** We all have gifts and talents that can be shared with others. We must be sure we are being kind as we help others learn something they may not know. Like Carl Walker and Grant West, we can help make a difference together.

- **Remember to "play an hour a day."** One of Grant West's greatest qualities was his dedication to his craft. His family encouraged him to practice daily, and that instilled a work ethic in him that allowed him to become a huge influencer of the development of music culture and education in the Twin Cities.

- **Don't be afraid to ask for help.** Teamwork makes the dream work. Grant West had a strong friendship with Carl Walker. The two friends shared the responsibility of running their music school. It is good to have someone we can lean on when we need some extra help in life.

- **Discover your roots.** Grant West did not know his history from a young age because the education in Wyoming did not teach about the accomplishments of Black people. He grew up believing that Black people did not contribute to the development or growth of any industry. After he grew up and left Cheyenne, he learned more about the incredible work, important accomplishments, and rich history of Black people. He learned that Black people served as the foundation upon which the United States was built.

ABOUT THE AUTHOR

Tristan Hitchens-Brookins is a law student at Michigan State University and a Law and Policy intern for Planting People Growing Justice. He grew up in Saint Paul, Minnesota. He wants to earn his law degree and serve his community in the field of immigration.

GLOSSARY

Affordable	Within a cost that is not too high
Business	A person's way of making money by exchanging goods and services
Critical Thinking	Serious time and focus used to solve a problem
Dedication	Spending time focusing on one topic
Jazz	A distinct style of American music with unique rhythms and abnormal accents that the musicians often create themselves
Leader	A person who commands a group of people
Segregation	The practice of separating different groups of people by race, gender, or class
Stenographer	A person whose job it is to write down the words people speak
Venue	A place where an event happens

SOURCE NOTES

Tyner, A. (2024, June 1). 6-1-24 Grant West Interview.

Hitchens-Brookins, T. (2024, July 6). 7-6-24 Grant West Interview.

WALKER | WEST. "About Us," 2024. https://walkerwest.org/about-us/.

BOOKS

Asim, J., & Polk, J. K. (2022). *A child's introduction to jazz: The musicians, culture, and roots of the world's coolest music.* Black Dog & Leventhal.

Erskine, K., & Palmer, C. (2017). *Mama Africa!: How Miriam Makeba spread hope with her song.* Farrar Straus Giroux.

Rockliff, M., & Wood, M. (2018). *Born to swing: Lil Hardin Armstrong's life in jazz.* Calkins Creek, an imprint of *Highlights.*

Weatherford, C. B., & Qualls, S. (2022). *Before John was a jazz giant: A song of John Coltrane.* Square Fish, an imprint of Macmillan Publishing Group, LLC.

WEBSITES

Burton, A. T. (n.d.). *Slave revolt of 1842.* Oklahoma Historical Society | OHS. https://www.okhistory.org/publications/enc/entry?entry=SL002#:~:text=Of%20the%20Five%20Tribes%2C%20the,as%20English%20interpreters%20and%20translators

Our Organization. Urban League Twin Cities. (n.d.). https://ultcmn.org/our-organization/

Sammy Davis Jr. Biography. (2021, April 20). https://www.biography.com/actors/sammy-davis-jr.

Schomburg Center for Research in Black Culture. The New York Public Library. (n.d.). https://www.nypl.org/locations/schomburg.

Tulsiani, R. (2024, February 14). *Embracing diversity in learning styles to personalize the experience.* eLearning Industry. https://elearningindustry.com/embracing-diversity-in-learning-styles-to-personalize-the-experience.

ABOUT PLANTING PEOPLE GROWING JUSTICE LEADERSHIP INSTITUTE

Planting People Growing Justice Leadership Institute seeks to plant seeds of social change through education, training, and community outreach.

A portion of the proceeds from this book will support the educational programming of Planting People Growing Justice Leadership Institute.